AlphaBasics

Musical Instruments

from A to Z

A Bobbie Kalman Book

🌳 Crabtree Publishing Company

www.crabtreebooks.com

Created by Bobbie Kalman

For Elvira Graci,
who sings like an angel

Editor-in-Chief
Bobbie Kalman

Managing editor
Lynda Hale

Editors
Niki Walker
Greg Nickles

Text and photo research
Tara Harte

Computer design
Lynda Hale

Production coordinator
Hannelore Sotzek

Consultant
Laura Thomas, Director
of the Niagara Symphony
Summer Camp

Separations and film
Dot 'n Line Image Inc.
CCS Princeton (cover)

Printer
Worzalla Publishing Company

Special thanks to
Marisa Berswick (the model who appears on the cover); the teachers and
children of the Niagara Symphony Summer Camp; Laura Thomas; Cynthia
Konopka; Judy Fuzzen; Laura Tilley, Executive Director of the Niagara
Symphony Association; John Lummen School of Music; Ridley College;
The Hogan Jazz Archive; The Shrine to Music Museum, University of South
Dakota; Ann Randall; Nicola Hill; Jessica Lindal; Gillian Buck; and Victoria
Village Public School
Every reasonable effort has been made to determine the names of children
pictured in this book. The publishers would be pleased to have any errors
or omissions brought to their attention so that they may be corrected in
subsequent printings.

Photographs and reproductions
Art Resource, NY: page 26 (detail); Marc Crabtree: title page, pages 12, 13; Erich
Lessing/Art Resource, NY: pages 19 (left: detail), 28 (detail); Giraudon/Art
Resource, NY: page 22 (detail); Hampton University Museum, Hampton, VA:
page 6 (detail); Bobbie Kalman: pages 9, 18 (right), 31 (top); Scala/Art
Resource, NY: pages 10 (detail), 15 (detail), 16 (detail); The Shrine to Music
Museum: page 18 (left); Victoria and Albert Museum, London/Art Resource,
NY: page 4 (detail); Jerry Whitaker: cover, pages 8 (top left), 21, 24 (bottom), 26,
29 (bottom); Other photographs by Image Club Graphics and Digital Vision

Illustrations
Barbara Bedell: pages 20, 25
Cori Marvin: pages 5 (all), 7, 11 (all), 21, 26, 27 (top), 30

Crabtree Publishing Company

PMB 16A
350 Fifth Avenue
Suite 3308
New York
N.Y. 10118

612 Welland Avenue
St. Catharines
Ontario, Canada
L2M 5V6

73 Lime Walk
Headington
Oxford OX3 7AD
United Kingdom

Cataloging in Publication Data
Kalman, Bobbie
    Musical Instruments from A to Z

(AlphaBasiCs)
Includes index.

ISBN 0-86505-378-2 (library bound) ISBN 0-86505-408-8 (pbk.)
This book is an alphabetical introduction to different types of
musical instruments, describing their origins and how to play them.

1. Musical instruments—Juvenile literature. 2. English language—
Alphabet—Juvenile literature. [1. Musical instruments. 2. Alphabet.]
I. Title. II. Series: Kalman, Bobbie. AlphaBasiCs

ML460.K27 1997   j784.19   LC 97 39982
                                                     CIP

Contents

is not for harps, but it has to do with harps. Harps have been around for thousands of years. They make a beautiful sound when you pluck their strings. Most people think of angels when they hear a harp. "Harp" does not start with A, but **angel music** does.

This large harp is a **pedal harp**. It has 68 strings. With their right hand, players pluck the strings that make the higher sounds. With their left hand, they pluck the low-sounding strings. Players can also pump the foot pedals to change the pitch.

Angle harps are very old. "Angle" means triangle in Greek. Can you guess why this harp was given its name?

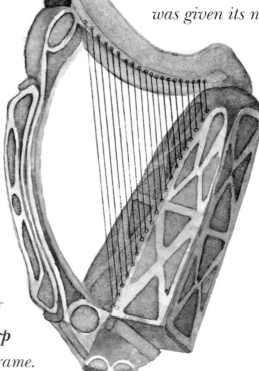

The strings of the **frame harp** are inside a frame.

is for an instrument with a round body and five strings. Players pluck or strum the strings. This instrument was brought to North America from Africa. For hundreds of years, it was part of African American folk music. Did you guess that B is for **banjo**?

Children learn folk music by listening to their parents play instruments and sing.

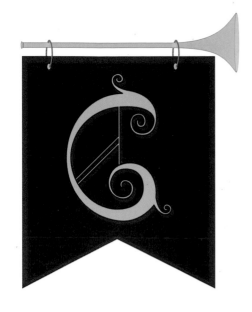

is for an instrument made of stones. The stones are carved in shapes such as fish, fruit, clouds, or bells. Each stone vibrates and makes a different sound when you strike it with a mallet. Did you know that the **ch'ing** is an instrument from China?

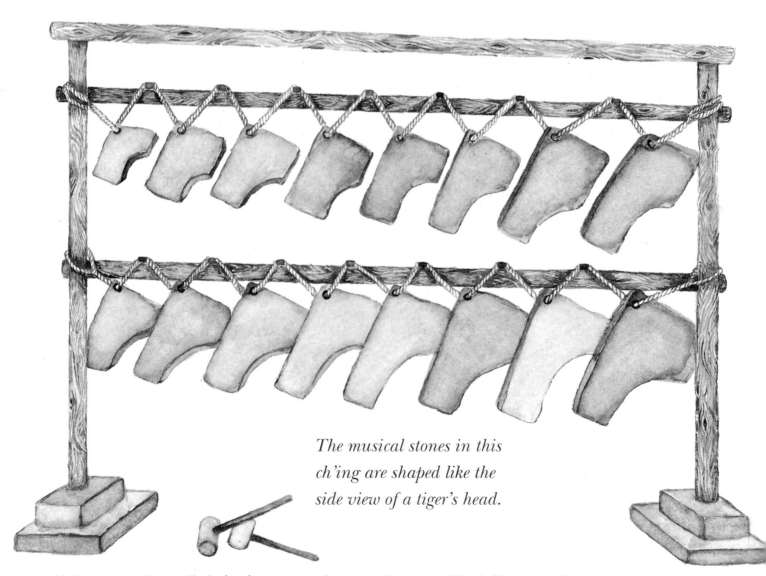

The musical stones in this ch'ing are shaped like the side view of a tiger's head.

*Ch'ings are also called **ringing stones** because they ring like bells when they are played.*

7

is for something you hit with your hands or sticks. It helps keep the beat of music. Native People say it sounds like the heartbeat of Mother Earth. In the past, people sent long-distance messages by playing it loud. Did you guess that D is for **drum**?

Timpani drums are very large and can sound just like thunder. BOOM! BOOM!

This goblet-shaped drum is called a **djembé**. *It is made of pottery or wood and played with the hands.*

Drum kits have several drums and cymbals and are played with sticks.

Indian **tabla drums** *are played with the hands.*

A Native American **frame drum** *is a stretched animal skin on a frame.*

is for a guitar that you can play really LOUDLY! You play a guitar with things that start with F. No, not your feet! You play an **electric** guitar with **fingers**!

*When you pluck or strum its strings, an electric guitar creates an electric **signal**. The signal travels through thick wires to an **amplifier**, which turns the signal into loud sound.*

is for an instrument like the one on page 9, but this one is not electric. This instrument usually has six strings but sometimes has four or twelve. You can pluck or strum the strings. When you play this instrument, people often sing along! Did you guess that G is for **guitar**?

*This man is playing a **Spanish guitar**, which is also known as a **classical guitar**. It has six strings. Most players pluck the strings rather than strum them.*

is for instruments that you blow. Long ago, people used them to call to one another. They made them from shells, wood, and something that grew on the head of some animals. Later on, these instruments were made of brass. Did you guess that H is for **horns**?

The **bugle** is a common brass horn. It was once used in hunting and for sending messages to soldiers during battle.

A **shofar** is a ram's horn. It is sounded to signal the Jewish New Year.

The **conch shell** is the earliest type of horn.

Alpenhorn means "horn of the Alps" in German. The Alps are a mountain chain found in some European countries, including Switzerland, Austria, and Germany. This long horn was made from a hollowed tree trunk. Its sound could be heard far away as it echoed through the mountains.

is for **instruments** you can make yourself. To make a banjo, panpipes, and maracas, you will need:

- a piece of wood
- 12 screws
- 6 rubber bands
- corrugated cardboard
- 6 - 8 straws
- 2 plastic bottles
- dried beans
- paints

The instructions are below.

Ask an adult to help you hammer and turn the screws into the wood. Stretch the rubber bands across them.

Cut the straws into different lengths. Place one in every second opening in the cardboard. Now blow!

Paint the bottles and let them dry. Drop the beans into them, screw on the caps, and shake, shake, shake!

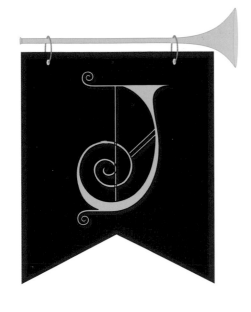

is for a noisy celebration. Now that you have finished making your instruments, it is time for some music! Invite your friends to play along with you. How many songs can you play? It does not matter how you sound, as long as you have fun **jamming** at your noisy **jamboree**!

is for an important part of many instruments. Pianos and accordions have one. Other instruments have two or even four! This musical thing has many black and white parts that give it its name. You press these keys with your fingers. Did you guess that K is for **keyboard**?

is for a stringed instrument whose name sounds like "flute." This instrument is like a guitar, but its pegbox is bent. The pegbox has pegs sticking out of it. Each string is wound around one peg. To tune a string, you turn its peg. Did you guess that this old instrument is a **lute**?

is for a word that is found in the title of this book. Hearing it can make people sing and dance. Composers hear it in their mind and then write it down so that other people can play or sing the sounds. Did you guess that M is for **music**?

This composer's name is Antonio Vivaldi. He lived and wrote music in the late 1600s and early 1700s. His music is still played today.

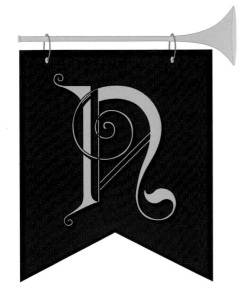

is for the symbols that are used to write music. They tell musicians what sounds to make with their instruments and when they should make them. They show when the sounds should be higher or lower and longer or shorter. Did you know that N is for **notes**?

*Notes are written on, above, or below five lines called a **staff**. Each line or space stands for a different sound. Notes on the bottom of the staff have a lower sound than those on the top.*

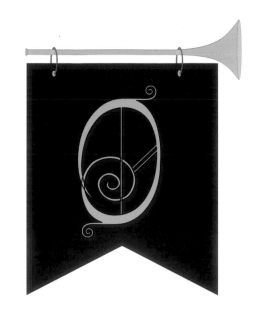

is for a keyboard instrument with pipes. When you press a key, air rushes into one or more pipes and makes a sound. Small pipes sound high notes, and large ones make deep notes. Players control which pipes are open and which are closed. Did you guess that O is for **organ**?

*There are two kinds of organ keyboards: **manuals** and **pedals**. Manuals are played with the hands, and pedals are played with the feet. Old organs, like the two shown here, have only one manual and no pedals. Many organs today have four manuals.*

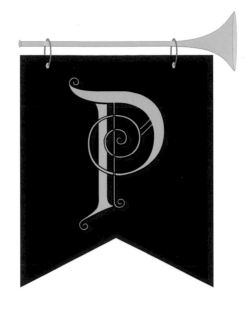

is for a family of keyboard instruments whose name is short for pianoforte. This name means "quiet-loud" in Italian. When a key is pressed softly, it makes a quiet sound. When it is hit hard, it makes a loud sound. Harpsichords are part of this family. Did you guess **piano family**?

*Many **harpsichords** cannot be played louder or softer. Their volume stays the same.*

***Grand pianos** have a rich, deep sound.*

*These girls are playing an **upright piano**.*

is for an instrument that is popular in the mountain regions of South America. People use it to play folk music. They blow into the mouthpiece and make different notes by covering the holes with their fingers. Did you guess that Q is for **quena**?

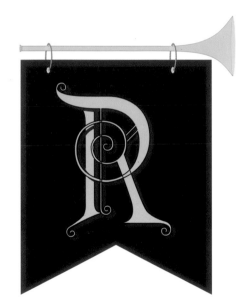

is for the family of instruments to which the quena belongs. Saxophones, clarinets, oboes, and bassoons are also in this family. A reed, which is made of one or two thin strips of cane or plastic, is inside the mouthpiece of each instrument. Did you know that R is for **reed instruments**?

reed

*The **oboe** is a double-reed instrument. It is known for its high, sad sound.*

When a player blows into a reed instrument, his or her breath makes the reed vibrate. These vibrations cause the air inside to make a sound.

The **saxophone** is named after Antoine Joseph Sax. The saxophone is the most important solo instrument in a jazz band.

Clarinets sound high and sweet. They are used in orchestras.

Bassoons produce deep sounds. In an orchestra, the bassoon players sit next to the clarinet players.

is for instruments with parts that are plucked, strummed, or struck. On some, players pull a bow across the front of the instrument to make a sound. Violins, guitars, and harps are all part of this family. Did you know that S is for **stringed instruments**?

*The woman on the right is playing an old **clavichord**. Its keyboard is on one side. When she presses the keys, small hammers inside the clavichord hit the strings. The cello on the left and the lute played by the man are also stringed instruments.*

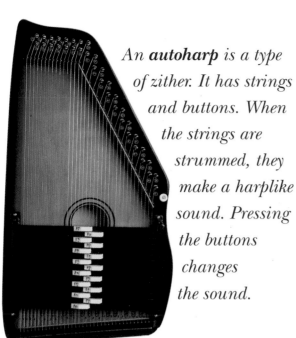

An **autoharp** is a type of zither. It has strings and buttons. When the strings are strummed, they make a harplike sound. Pressing the buttons changes the sound.

Bouzoukis are lutes from Greece. The strings are grouped in pairs.

A **bandura** is a combination of a lute and zither. Find these instruments on other pages of this book.

Russian **balalaikas** have three strings. Most musicians play one string at a time.

Mandolins are like lutes. They are played by plucking the strings with a **plectrum**, or pick.

A violin is played by pulling the bow across its strings.

T is for three instruments that are made of a metal called brass. These three instruments, plus the French horn, make up part of the brass section of an orchestra. Did you guess that T is for **trombone**, **trumpet**, and **tuba**?

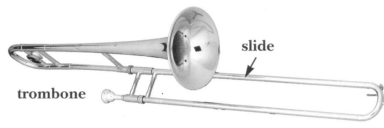

trombone

slide

*The **French horn** can make a wider variety of sounds than the other horns in the brass family.*

*To play different notes on a trombone, players move a **slide**.*

To make a sound on a brass instrument, a person blows into the mouthpiece while buzzing his or her lips.

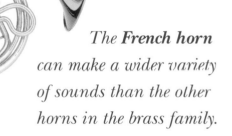

tuba

To play different notes on a tuba or trumpet, players press valves.

valves

24

trumpet

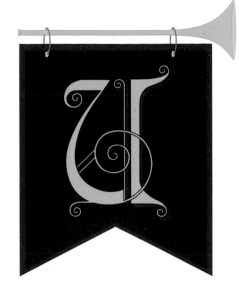

is for an instrument whose name means "jumping flea" in Hawaiian. It has four strings and looks like a small guitar. It is easy to play. Players strum it lightly with their fingers. In Hawaii, people play it to accompany hula dancers. Did you know that this small guitar is a **ukulele**?

You can also play a ukulele with a pick.

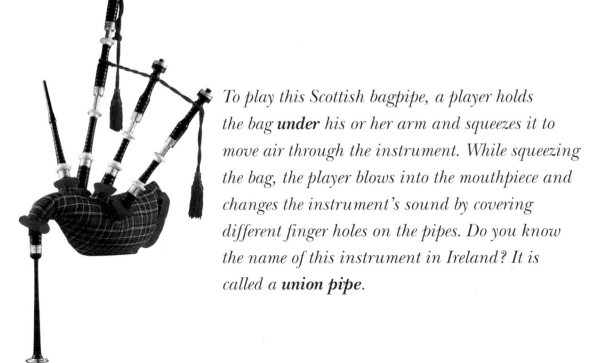

*To play this Scottish bagpipe, a player holds the bag **under** his or her arm and squeezes it to move air through the instrument. While squeezing the bag, the player blows into the mouthpiece and changes the instrument's sound by covering different finger holes on the pipes. Do you know the name of this instrument in Ireland? It is called a **union pipe**.*

is for a family of stringed instruments that are played with a bow. These instruments have similar shapes but different sizes. There are cellos, double basses, violas, and violins in this family. Did you guess that these instruments belong to the **violin family**?

cello

The **violin** is the smallest member of its family. It is thought to be the most important instrument in an orchestra. The violin, like the viola, tucks easily under the player's chin.

The **viola** looks like a violin, but it is larger. It has a lower, warmer sound than the violin.

The **double bass** is the largest member of the violin family. The player stands behind it and holds it upright. The double bass is often taller than the person playing it!

Players must sit on a chair to play the **cello**, which is the second-largest instrument in the violin family. The cello rests on a metal spike.

is for instruments that use air to make their sound. Some have a mouthpiece into or across which players blow air. Others have a bag or bellows that squeezes air through the instrument. Did you guess that these instruments are **wind instruments**?

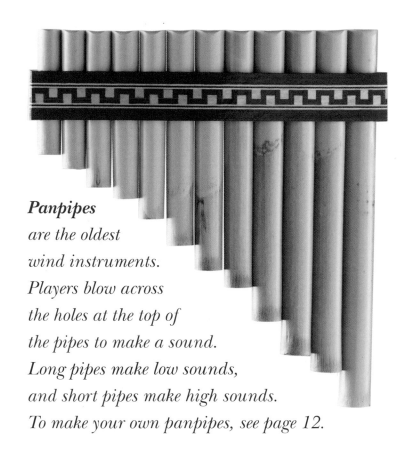

Panpipes
are the oldest
wind instruments.
Players blow across
the holes at the top of
the pipes to make a sound.
Long pipes make low sounds,
and short pipes make high sounds.
To make your own panpipes, see page 12.

Recorders are whistle
flutes. In the past, they
were made of wood.
Today most are plastic.
They are very popular
in schools.

Saxophones, clarinets, and oboes are also
wind instruments. (See pages 20-21.) There
are many other types of wind instruments
in this book. How many can you find?

A **side-blown flute**, shown here
and on the opposite page, has its
mouthpiece to one side. Players
hold the instrument to one side
of their body.

is for an instrument that has two rows of wooden bars. Each bar is a different size and makes a different sound when you tap it with a mallet. This instrument is a type of percussion instrument, which is played by being struck. Did you know that X is for **xylophone**?

To play a xylophone, you strike the bars with a pair of plastic or metal mallets.

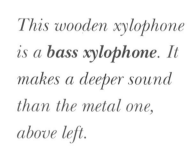

*This wooden xylophone is a **bass xylophone**. It makes a deeper sound than the metal one, above left.*

*The **marimba** is a type of xylophone that also makes a low sound. In the past, marimbas were made of wooden slabs with gourds underneath. The vibrating gourds made the sound louder.*

is for **yam stick**. A yam stick is a simple stick that helps Australian Aboriginal dancers keep the beat. One girl is using a stick to beat a **slit drum**. The other is playing a **rain stick**. It has seeds inside. When you turn it from end to end, the falling seeds sound like raindrops.

The name of the instrument to the right is easy. It starts with Z. Did you guess it's a **zeze**? A zeze is also called a thumb piano.

*Players push down on the metal parts, called **plates**, with their fingers and thumbs. When a plate springs up, it sounds similar to hitting one piano key at a time.*

Words to Know

amplifier A device that makes sound louder

classical guitar A guitar with six strings and a wide neck

composer A person who writes music

ensemble A small group of musicians who perform together

jamboree A noisy or festive gathering or celebration

jamming Playing an instrument for fun

keyboard A set of keys as on a piano

keys Buttons or levers on an instrument that are pressed to make sound

pitch In music, the high or low quality of sound

plectrum A small, thin piece of metal, plastic, or bone used to pluck strings on an instrument

signal A flow of electricity between an electric instrument and an amplifier, which is changed into sound

slide Tubing on a trombone used to change notes

staff The five horizontal lines and four spaces on which musical notes are arranged

valves Devices in brass wind instruments that, when pressed, change the sound

vibrate To move rapidly back and forth or up and down

Index

4 5 6 7 8 9 0 Printed in the U.S.A. 6 5 4 3 2